Late Company

Also by Jordan Tannahill

Age of Minority: Three Solo Plays
Concord Floral
Declarations
Liminal
Theatre of the Unimpressed: In Search of Vital Drama
The Videofag Book (edited with William Ellis)

Late Company

A *play by* Jordan Tannahill

Playwrights Canada Press
Toronto

For professional or amateur production rights, please contact:
Colin Rivers, Marquis Entertainment
312-73 Richmond St. W., Toronto, ON M5H 4E8
416.960.9123, info@marquisent.ca, www.marquisent.ca

LIBRARY AND ARCHIVES CANADA CATALOGUING IN PUBLICATION
Tannahill, Jordan, author
      Late company : a play / by Jordan Tannahill. -- Second edition.

Issued in print and electronic formats.
ISBN 978-1-77091-897-9 (softcover).--ISBN 978-1-77091-898-6 (PDF).
--ISBN 978-1-77091-899-3 (EPUB).--ISBN 978-1-77091-900-6 (Kindle)

      I. Title.

PS8639.A577L38 2018   C812'.6   C2017-907060-6
                                                  C2017-907061-4

Playwrights Canada Press acknowledges that we operate on land which, for thousands of years, has been the traditional territories of the Mississaugas of the New Credit, the Huron-Wendat, the Anishinaabe, Métis, and the Haudenosaunee peoples. Today, this meeting place is still home to many Indigenous people from across Turtle Island and we are grateful to have the opportunity to work and play here.

We acknowledge the financial support of the Canada Council for the Arts—which last year invested $153 million to bring the arts to Canadians throughout the country—the Ontario Arts Council (OAC), the Ontario Media Development Corporation, and the Government of Canada for our publishing activities.

Canada Council for the Arts / Conseil des arts du Canada

ONTARIO ARTS COUNCIL
CONSEIL DES ARTS DE L'ONTARIO
an Ontario government agency
un organisme du gouvernement de l'Ontario

Canada

Ontario
Ontario Media Development Corporation

For sissy boys everywhere

Late Company was first produced by Suburban Beast and surface/underground at the SummerWorks Performance Festival, August 9–18, 2013, with the following cast and crew:

Debora Shaun-Hastings: Rosemary Dunsmore
Michael Shaun-Hastings: Richard Greenblatt
Tamara Dermot: Fiona Highet
Bill Dermot: Paul Fauteux
Curtis Dermot: Mark Correia

Directed by Peter Pasyk
Produced by Naomi Skwarna
Stage management by Emilie Aubin
Set and lighting design by Patrick Lavender

The play was subsequently produced by Touchstone Theatre, Vancouver, in 2014; the Manitoba Theatre Centre, Winnipeg, in 2015; and by surface/underground and Why Not Theatre at the Theatre Centre, Toronto, in 2015.

Late Company was first performed in Europe at the Finborough Theatre, London, on April 25, 2017, and later transferred to Trafalgar Studios, London, on August 21, 2017. It featured the following cast and crew:

Debora Shaun-Hastings: Lucy Robinson
Michael Shaun-Hastings: Todd Boyce
Tamara Dermot: Lisa Stevenson
Bill Dermot: Alex Lowe
Curtis Dermot: David Leopold

Directed by Michael Yale
Set and costume design by Zahra Mansouri
Lighting design by Nic Farman
Sound design by Christopher Prosho

Characters

Michael Shaun-Hastings: fifty-three, male
Debora Shaun-Hastings: fifty-two, female
Tamara Dermot: forty-six, female
Bill Dermot: forty-nine, male
Curtis Dermot: seventeen, male

Setting

A tastefully appointed living room and dining room in an
upper-middle-class suburban home. Present day.

Playwright's Note

Directors should feel at liberty to update specific cultural and
geographic references in the script to suit the year and locale of
production.

Lights up on the Shaun-Hastings busily preparing their formally set dining-room table.

DEBORA
Unbelievable.

MICHAEL
Don't—

DEBORA
No: painfully predictable.

MICHAEL
He called.

DEBORA
Forty minutes ago.

MICHAEL
We're still getting ready.

DEBORA
No, this is fussing.

MICHAEL
I'm not—

DEBORA
Now it looks overdone.

She holds up the napkins.

These rings are too formal.

MICHAEL
Formal's good. It's the music.

DEBORA
The music is appropriate.

MICHAEL
For a Mayan sacrifice.

DEBORA
It's contemplative.

MICHAEL
Welcome to our house. Now lie down on this plinth while we cut out
your heart.

Beat.

They're probably lost in the labyrinth.

DEBORA
The roads are not that twisty.

Beat.

Besides, they have a GPS. I saw it in their car. Well it's not a car; it's one of those horrible Ford Escape mini-tanks. I've seen it in the school parking lot. Their licence plate has their surname on it.

MICHAEL
No.

DEBORA
Yes.

MICHAEL
Ridiculous.

DEBORA
They have a GPS on their dash. So no excuse.

MICHAEL
So they have money. For some reason I thought they'd be—you know—I just have this image of her sitting on the couch, shouting at her kids. Is she fat?

DEBORA
I don't think so. Janice tells me they go to the same GoodLife.

MICHAEL
Hockey parents too, I'm assuming. With a truck like that.

DEBORA
Okay, okay—let's just—

MICHAEL
Right.

DEBORA
Clear the negativity.

MICHAEL
(deep breath) It's going . . . *(deep breath)* It's gone.

DEBORA
We want this.

MICHAEL
Can you imagine if I punched him in the face? Giant uppercut under the chin.

DEBORA
We're receiving and bestowing, Michael.

MICHAEL
I know—

DEBORA
Receive and bestow.

MICHAEL
But if he says anything snarky I'll bestow him an uppercut.

They continue arranging, fidgeting for a moment in silence.

DEBORA
We were hockey parents. For a couple winters.

MICHAEL

Oh those were glorified skating lessons. He was five.

DEBORA

Shh. There it is again.

She moves to the stereo and turns down the music.

The knocking.

MICHAEL

I can't hear anything.

DEBORA

Why do you never hear it? It always sounds like someone's upstairs.

MICHAEL

Do you want me to check?

DEBORA

Don't be silly.

MICHAEL

Are we sure about this?

DEBORA

I know there's no one there.

MICHAEL

About tonight.

DEBORA

Of course we're sure.

MICHAEL

We have one way that we've envisioned this going. Which is constructive. But it might, really, not be.

DEBORA

Well obviously that's a possibility.

MICHAEL

And are we prepared for that? For a complete unmitigated disaster. Should we have a—a signal? Like a—

DEBORA

An ejection seat?

MICHAEL

Exactly. Like if things are—if one of us gets overwhelmed or if we just need space, to leave the room, should we have some kind of—

DEBORA

A safety.

MICHAEL

Something subtle.

DEBORA

Hmm. What if—

The doorbell rings.

Shit.

MICHAEL

No, no, not shit. We're happy to see them.

DEBORA
What if we—

MICHAEL
Forget it, forget it.

> *MICHAEL moves to the door and answers it.* TAMARA, BILL, *and their son,* CURTIS *Dermot, stand in the door in their winter jackets.* TAMARA *holds a pie and* BILL *holds a bottle of wine.*

You made it!

TAMARA
Sorry we're late.

BILL
We kept getting turned around. It's a winding kinda area, eh?

MICHAEL
Oh yeah, really loopy. Everyone gets lost.

DEBORA
Not everyone.

MICHAEL
Lots of people.

TAMARA
Should've brought one of those blood-sniffer dogs or something.

DEBORA
Or sent up some flares.

DEBORA takes the wine and the pie. She notices a piece of paper in
TAMARA's hand.

TAMARA

Oh this is the— Did you want to take this, or—?

DEBORA

No you can hold on to that. *(holding up pie)* Yummy . . .

TAMARA

It's from that Polish farmer's market near the school. Do you know it?
Real nifty spot.

BILL

It was in the news for selling raw milk.

MICHAEL

(overlapping; hanging up peoples' coats) I can grab your coats there—

DEBORA

(overlapping) I heard about that. That farmer on trial—

TAMARA

I mean, it's not like it's breast milk for heaven's sake! Let us drink it raw
if we want to, am I right? Lovely place you have here.

BILL

(holding out his hand to MICHAEL) I'm Bill by the way.

MICHAEL *and* BILL *shake hands.*

TAMARA

Here I'm acting like we already know each other. I'm Tamara obviously,
and this is Curtis.

MICHAEL
Hi Curtis. I'm Michael.

CURTIS
Hi.

CURTIS and MICHAEL shake hands

DEBORA
And I'm Debora.

She shakes their hands. MICHAEL leads them into the living room.

TAMARA
Really lovely place.

MICHAEL
Welcome to the party.

DEBORA
Can I get you something? Wine, beer?

BILL
Just water for us, thanks.

TAMARA
Just a calorie thing, nothing religious.

DEBORA
Curtis?

CURTIS
Milk, if you have it. Please.

DEBORA
We only drink breast milk, is that okay?

CURTIS
What?

DEBORA
I'm kidding. We have the regular kind.

CURTIS
Whatever. Thanks.

> *DEBORA exits into the kitchen. BILL notices the pennant on MICHAEL's wall.*

BILL
We share alma maters, Michael.

MICHAEL
Really, what'd you take at Queen's?

BILL
Did my M.B.A. there.

MICHAEL
Get out, so did I. Class of '83.

BILL
Class of '87.

MICHAEL
You're just a kid.

BILL
Did you know a guy named Ruben—oh what's his—Ruben Talbot?

MICHAEL
Sounds familiar.

BILL
Big black guy. Footballer type.

MICHAEL
Nope.

BILL
You play any ball there?

MICHAEL
No. Not sure why I have that on the wall really. Bit of a poser I suppose.

TAMARA
Bill played rugby.

MICHAEL
Oh yeah?

TAMARA
Paying for it now, though.

MICHAEL
You play any sports, Curtis?

CURTIS
Hockey.

MICHAEL
Yeah? Competitively?

CURTIS
Used to.

TAMARA
We withdrew him this winter. He was having trouble focusing in class. I think there was a bit of an emotional toll.

MICHAEL
It can be a rough sport.

TAMARA
I mean from all of this.

MICHAEL
Joel, you mean?

TAMARA
Hun?

CURTIS shrugs.

It's just been a number of things.

DEBORA returns with the drinks.

Jeez, here I am just sitting on my butt. Can I give you a hand?

DEBORA
No, no, on your butt's just where we like you.

TAMARA
Steven and Chris, right?

DEBORA
Sorry?

TAMARA
How you did your drapes like that with the ribbons. Did you get that from *Steven and Chris*?

DEBORA
Is that a store?

TAMARA
It's a show on CBC; they're partners. Both decorators and they're a real hoot. Even Bill will watch from time to time—

   BILL puts his hands up to admit guilt.

DEBORA
It's something I learned from my mother.

MICHAEL
Deb tells me you have three girls.

TAMARA
All at Waterloo.

MICHAEL
All three, wow.

BILL
All pre-law.

MICHAEL

Pre-law. What is that, like English?

DEBORA

All spitting images of their mother.

MICHAEL

You've met them.

DEBORA

No, Tam sent me a photo.

MICHAEL

Oh. You never showed me.

TAMARA

The one in the backyard? Yeah, that's a nice one of them.

MICHAEL

How come you never showed me?

DEBORA

We've had a really nice correspondence.

TAMARA

Well, it's just so funny: after everything that happened I gave my email address to Mr. Pasternack, the principal, to pass along to Debora; you know, one mother to another—

MICHAEL

I know how it started.

TAMARA

Well I was expecting—I'm not sure what I was expecting. Certainly not Deb. She was just so warm. I felt like I was talking to this long-lost friend. We talked about being moms; we exchanged some photos—

MICHAEL

(to DEBORA) Which photos did you send?

TAMARA

—and then it came out we were reading the same book, *Attracting Positivity.*

DEBORA

Raj Gupta. The orange cover.

MICHAEL

I know.

TAMARA

I mean we were just both in the same headspace. There's a word for that.

DEBORA

Synergy.

TAMARA

That's it! And in the book he talks about having a conversation with your loss. And wasn't it Deb who said, "Well maybe we should do this."

MICHAEL

Deb's put a lot of thought into this. I just did the appetizers.

MICHAEL exits into the kitchen.

TAMARA

Sure you don't need a hand?

DEBORA

It's all done.

TAMARA

I know how much work goes into pulling one of these together.

DEBORA

Well it's not like I have anything else to do.

TAMARA

But I'd imagine your artwork must be fairly time-consuming.

DEBORA

Right. Well . . .

BILL

What sort of thing do you do?

DEBORA

Steel, mostly.

TAMARA

Suppose that's the "postmodern" thing, right? Your idea is my idea.

DEBORA

I do metal work.

BILL

Are those yours there?

DEBORA
They are.

TAMARA
Fantastic.

DEBORA
(referring to a fist-shaped sculpture) That one there is called *Thatcher.*

BILL
Right. Iron fist, velvet glove.

DEBORA
I like to think of my work as portraiture.

TAMARA
(referring to a rather phallic-shaped sculpture) And that one?

DEBORA
That one's called *Daddy.*

> *TAMARA nods.*

TAMARA
My mother was an artist.

BILL
Sleeping with Leonard Cohen does not make her an artist.

TAMARA
She did watercolours.

BILL
She was a hobbyist.

TAMARA

Why are you diminishing it?

BILL

She wasn't an "artist"; she didn't make a living at it.

TAMARA

(to DEBORA) But you also teach. At the university.

BILL

I was surprised when she told me, actually. You being married to a Conservative politician, it seems a little, well—

DEBORA

Antithetical.

BILL

Exactly.

DEBORA

One moment you're dating the president of student council and the next you're a campaign wife.

TAMARA

Does it make it hard to be creative?

DEBORA

It makes it hard to be righteous.

   Beat.

A lot of my early work was about power structures. Primarily about being ground under them. And now we are the power, aren't we? I mean that's what it looks like from the outside at least. No matter how powerless we may actually feel.

MICHAEL returns with the appetizers.

TAMARA
Yum, that looks— Oh, is that shrimp? I'm afraid Curtis has a very serious shellfish allergy.

DEBORA
Oh no, really?

TAMARA
Yeah, really swollen throat—

CURTIS
It's fatal.

DEBORA
I didn't know.

TAMARA
I thought I told you in our emails.

DEBORA
No.

TAMARA
I could have sworn—

DEBORA
I asked about allergies—

TAMARA
It's something I always tell people.

DEBORA
I made cream pasta with scallops. I'm assuming that's a problem.

TAMARA
Yeah, that's going to be a problem. But Curtis can eat some cheese and bread and some, maybe some fruit.

DEBORA
That's really too bad—

TAMARA
No, its fine, he's very used to it. He's very sensitive to a lot of things actually. Even latex.

BILL
Watch out, ladies!

> BILL *laughs towards* MICHAEL, *but desists when he doesn't get a reaction.*

TAMARA
I think it's the antibacterial soap they pushed on us all those years—

BILL
We never had antibacterial—

TAMARA
The daycares did.

MICHAEL
Or the plastics in everything.

TAMARA

Well then there's that too.

BILL

You oughta make a private member's bill!

TAMARA

On soap? Don't be ridiculous.

CURTIS

You look just like your lawn-sign photo. Which is good. I mean, 'cause politicians never look as good as their lawn-sign photos.

BILL

You got my vote last year.

TAMARA

Mine too.

BILL

And that's saying something; I mean, we've been Liberal for years.

TAMARA

Years.

BILL

If my father knew I voted Tory, he'd be just— *(gestures)* Rolling.

TAMARA

But then there're just no more viable options on the left, is there?

BILL

But you've always been a Red Tory, am I right?

MICHAEL
Is that the word around town?

DEBORA
It's not an unfair assessment.

BILL
I mean you were running downtown for years before they moved you out here. It's a totally different ball game down there.

MICHAEL
We were ready to move. The conditions were right.

BILL
Well obviously: you're in Parliament.

MICHAEL
I didn't move to get elected.

BILL
It certainly didn't hurt.

TAMARA
Bill—

BILL
I'm just speaking openly. That's the perception.

TAMARA
I'm sure it was very hard to leave your old neighbourhood after all those years. Pull Joel out of school, away from his friends.

MICHAEL
Joel didn't mind the move.

TAMARA
Still, he would have been more in his element downtown, no?

DEBORA
He always hated it out here.

MICHAEL
He didn't mind the change; he *liked* change.

Pause.

TAMARA
I just want to apologize again for being so late. I feel like we've started things off on the wrong foot and I, I just want to, to clear the air so we can really . . . focus on coming together tonight. I, we, just want you both to know that we feel very . . . fortunate . . . to be here. Don't we?

BILL
Absolutely.

CURTIS nods.

TAMARA
The truth is we were late because we were having a bit of a fight.

BILL
Tam—

TAMARA
And, well I think if we're to be open and honest with each other tonight—Bill had reservations—I would say pretty serious reservations—about all this.

BILL

I was just expressing some doubt. But I'm here, and I'm / happy to—

DEBORA

About what?

BILL

Well. Whether this would be a . . . whether this would be something beneficial. For all of us.

DEBORA

Pretty eleventh hour, no?

BILL

I don't know why Tam brought it up.

TAMARA

Because I want them to know that we're all coming at this from different angles and it's hard for everyone and to just acknowledge that. And to let you know why we were late.

DEBORA

You sure you don't want any wine?

TAMARA

Maybe just a splash.

> DEBORA *fills her glass.*

BILL

The guac's great.

DEBORA

It's all Michael.

MICHAEL

Easiest thing in the world to make.

BILL

She's got you in the kitchen?

MICHAEL

I like to cook.

DEBORA

Me, if it doesn't come in a box, it's not worth my time.

BILL

I took Tam to dinner last week. Eighty-five bucks for the meal. And if we didn't get the measliest little portions of—what was it, duck?

TAMARA

They just gouge you.

BILL

Probably saw us getting out of the car and said: "Oh here come a bunch of bozos." Seven leaves—I could count the leaves in my salad. And you get some chumps who just gush as if being ripped off changed their friggin' lives.

DEBORA

Should I start pulling dinner together?

MICHAEL

We don't have to rush.

DEBORA

Well it's a bit later than usual.

BILL
I'm easy.

DEBORA
I sense we want to get down to it, am I right? What we all came for.

TAMARA
Curtis?

CURTIS
Sure.

DEBORA
I think over dinner would be best.

    DEBORA *leaves for the kitchen.*

TAMARA
(exits into the kitchen after her) All right, this time I'm not asking—

MICHAEL
Who're you texting?

CURTIS
Just a girl.

MICHAEL
Your girlfriend?

    CURTIS *shrugs.*

BILL
Don't be a smartass.

CURTIS
It's complicated.

BILL
Don't worry, he doesn't even tell us about her.

MICHAEL
You'd make a great mime. Tell me something about yourself.

Beat.

CURTIS
I like comedy.

BILL
He and his buddies started making these comedy videos online. You probably know what I mean.

MICHAEL
Not really.

BILL
Oh they're a riot. There's one, the one about the convenience-store clerk; I mean some people might find it a bit offensive but the first time I saw it I literally died laughing.

CURTIS
Not literally.

BILL
I did!

CURTIS
If you literally died you'd be dead right now.

MICHAEL
So you like English as well.

CURTIS
(to BILL) Can I go to Julie's after this?

BILL
We'll see how late this goes.

MICHAEL
(pointing to phone) Is that Julie?

> *Beat.*

Was she in the same class as you and Joel?

CURTIS
Yeah.

MICHAEL
What did she think of Joel?

CURTIS
Nothing much. I don't know. Can we just leave her out of this?

BILL
Guess politics has you on the road a lot, eh?

MICHAEL
Some, yes.

BILL
A lot of events.

MICHAEL

It's always something. Which is hard because you don't always make it home for dinner. I've eaten samosas and latkes in every community centre in this city.

BILL

You're in Ottawa a lot?

MICHAEL

Most weekdays.

BILL

Weekend dad.

MICHAEL

I get back more than you'd think.

BILL

Porter's great.

MICHAEL

Yup.

BILL

Must've been hard on Joel growing up.

MICHAEL

Perhaps. Yes.

BILL

Were you two close?

MICHAEL

As close as parents and teens get. He's always been closer with his mother.

BILL

I had my own business for a while and I just found I was working 24-7. There was one night I came home and Curtis had had a band recital that day and I didn't even know he played an instrument. Tam said to me, "He's been playing the alto for six months." I had no idea!

CURTIS

Alto sax.

BILL

What?

CURTIS

There's no instrument called the alto.

BILL

Alto sax, yeah, I know. So I said, "You know what, it's not worth it." The kids were still young. I found a good nine-to-five with TD, and I haven't regretted it for a second.

MICHAEL

And Tamara?

BILL

She was able to stay home with the kids.

MICHAEL

That's rare.

BILL
It was important to us.

MICHAEL
I made time for Joel. Just so you know.

BILL
Good.

MICHAEL
He knew he could always come to me.

BILL
I'm glad to hear it.

MICHAEL
You don't sound convinced.

BILL
Are you trying to convince me?

MICHAEL
I was not just some weekend dad.

>   *Beat.*

.I turned down a cabinet post because it would have had me travelling
too much.

BILL
The party's been supportive.

MICHAEL
Of course they have.

BILL

Well you never know, especially with some of those backbenchers.

MICHAEL

This is my son we're talking about.

BILL

I think them releasing that "It Gets Better" video—that was quite smart.

MICHAEL

Smart?

BILL

I mean they couldn't have said nothing.

MICHAEL

I thought it was very touching. Deb and I were touched.

BILL

That's nice.

MICHAEL

It was.

BILL

Personally, I prefer to grieve in private.

MICHAEL

If my party wants to put together an "It Gets Better" video or walk in the Pride parade or wear pink ties in Question Period, that's their prerogative.

BILL

I can tell you want to do this about as much as I do.

MICHAEL
It's still very raw for me.

BILL
Women love to talk about everything. Everything out on the table. I'm very skeptical about all this stuff. Books that tell you how to grieve. I don't believe in plans of action. I think you deal with it alone and you deal with it until you're dead. And trust me, I've lost people very close to me before. I don't believe in closure. But that's just me.

MICHAEL
I'm not expecting a miracle, Bill. I'm just here to represent my son's best interests.

BILL
That makes two of us.

CURTIS
Can I go for a smoke?

BILL
You can wait.

CURTIS
I need some fresh air.

BILL
Then you shouldn't be smoking.

CURTIS
It'll help calm me down.

MICHAEL
Personally, I think it sounds like a great idea.

CURTIS

You can have one of mine if you'd like.

BILL

Devil on the shoulder, eh?

The men begin putting on their boots.

MICHAEL

Deb? *(calling)* Debora?

DEBORA

(offstage) What?

MICHAEL

Just going to show these guys the deck.

The men exit.

DEBORA

(offstage) We're about to eat!

MICHAEL

(offstage) Five minutes!

DEBORA

(offstage) It's not even shovelled!

DEBORA and TAMARA enter with several of the dinner dishes.

TAMARA

The more you tell them not to, the more they do it.

DEBORA

I got Michael to quit two campaigns ago. More or less. He just couldn't keep up.

TAMARA

They always have perfect timing, don't they? Just as things are ready to go.

DEBORA

Around here it's every man for himself. I just keep the freezer stocked.

TAMARA

You know, for me there's nothing more sacred than dinner. When the kids were still at home it was the only time we'd all be together. And they knew it was important so they didn't miss it.

    DEBORA tops up both their wine glasses.

DEBORA

Oops, slip of the hand.

TAMARA

I feel like I really get you, Deb.

DEBORA

There's not much to get.

TAMARA

And your art—it must make your life so rich.

    Beat.

When does an idea really excite you? I mean enough to say, "Okay now *there's* a sculpture."

DEBORA

God. I feel like I haven't felt that in ages.

TAMARA

Where artists come up with the things they do, it's just totally fascinating to me. Like Curtis with his comedy; where he gets it all I just don't know. He's really much more outgoing at home; I wish you could see that side of him.

DEBORA

He probably feels a little under the microscope tonight.

TAMARA

I know you probably have this one vision of him. And I can understand why you would. But he's really such a sweet kid. And funny, really funny, when he gets going.

DEBORA

Did you know what was happening?

TAMARA

Well I always knew that Curtis was in the sort of— You know, that he and his friends carried a lot of weight at the school. They thought they were pretty cool, pretty tough, but you know, when you're a mom you see through that. You see your baby just—pretending.

DEBORA

Why was he pretending?

TAMARA

Just putting on a bit of a macho-guy act. Maybe to prove something to himself; I don't know. Sometimes he'd bring it home and I'd tell him to cut it out. You know, using language that I don't approve of. I wasn't a fan of all of his friends. But I knew their parents and they were good people.

DEBORA

Did he show signs of it? As a child?

TAMARA

You mean like burning ants with magnifying glasses? No.

DEBORA

With other kids. In elementary school.

TAMARA

Actually he was pretty withdrawn when he was younger. He's really come out of his shell in high school.

DEBORA

And pushed others back into theirs.

TAMARA

What he did was cruel. But I don't think he's a cruel person.

DEBORA

And you can make that distinction?

TAMARA

I have to.

Pause.

Did you ever feel . . . Sometimes when I was holding him as a baby he felt like a stack of blank paper I could just write anything on. It was just like that fear you have before starting a letter, before you start writing, and you're worried it'll get away on you. But with a baby you can't— you can't just crumple up a baby and start again now, can you? I was so scared holding him. That he was going to get away on me.

Beat.

DEBORA
Funny. I never had that.

The men re-enter laughing, MICHAEL carrying the rest of the dinner, including CURTIS's special meal.

BILL
It's too bad you let those hedges get away on you. If you don't trim cedars every year, you end up with a bunch of sticks.

MICHAEL
We just don't make the time.

BILL
You behaving yourselves?

DEBORA
Is that going to be enough food for you?

CURTIS
Yeah, that's great.

BILL
He eats like a bird. We should get Curtis over on a weekend to help you wrangle them in. He does our hedges.

DEBORA
Well we hardly care; we're never out there.

Everyone finds a seat at the table.

TAMARA

Oh look, we have too many place settings.

DEBORA

One of them's for Joel.

BILL

The Polish do that; set places for the dead. My grandmother did that.

TAMARA

Do you do grace?

DEBORA

Do you?

TAMARA

No.

MICHAEL

Thank god.

> *They begin passing around the food.*

DEBORA

Careful, it's hot.

TAMARA

Should we put some on Joel's plate?

MICHAEL

Let's not get silly.

DEBORA

Are we getting too silly for you?

MICHAEL

Putting food on Joel's plate, yes.

TAMARA

Just thought I'd ask.

DEBORA

(to MICHAEL) Do you have our letter?

CURTIS

Did you want to do that now?

TAMARA

Let's wait until after dinner maybe.

BILL

Noticed you don't have any pictures of Joel up anywhere.

DEBORA

Guess we're not a family photo kind of family.

TAMARA

God we were a little insufferable with the camera, weren't we? Our own little Library and Archives of the kids.

MICHAEL

We sort of fell down in that department.

TAMARA

You ever make a sculpture of him, Deb?

DEBORA

What?

TAMARA
A sculpture of Joel.

DEBORA
I did once actually, yes.

MICHAEL
She wasn't happy with it.

DEBORA
I've always been better at portraits of people I don't know.

TAMARA
Sort of counterintuitive.

DEBORA
I suppose.

MICHAEL
I think we still have it in our basement.

DEBORA
It's in a bunch of pieces.

    Beat.

It was always on the to-do list though.

TAMARA
Art must be a real source of comfort for you.

DEBORA
Mostly I find it devastating.

TAMARA

Oh. When my mother died I just—I just tapped into this creative side of myself that had been sleeping. It's like I shook it awake and said, "Okay, I need you now!"

DEBORA

Losing one's mother is not the same as losing your teenage son.

TAMARA

Well loss is loss.

DEBORA

A woman dying of old age is natural; the death of a teenager is . . .

TAMARA

It was very painful for me.

DEBORA

I'm sure it was, but you can't compare the two. They're not comparable.

MICHAEL

Seems like you're the one comparing.

TAMARA

My point was about having strategies. Coping strategies. I needed to keep myself occupied. So I started doing handicrafts. Crocheting, quilting—

BILL

Everyone got a quilt for Christmas that year.

TAMARA

I went through a scarf phase. A sock phase.

MICHAEL

A sock phase.

TAMARA

It felt like I was knitting out my pain. Like that fairy tale about that little man who spins the hay into golden threads.

CURTIS

Rumpelstiltskin.

TAMARA

Maybe you'll pick up your sculpting again.

DEBORA

I don't want to turn my art into therapy.

BILL

Joel was a creative guy, wasn't he?

MICHAEL

Oh yeah. Dramatic.

TAMARA

I remember he was in *Midsummer Night's Dream*. Guess that was grade nine. I did some volunteer ushering.

MICHAEL

I think I was away for that one.

TAMARA

Who did he play again?

CURTIS

Oberon.

TAMARA

That's right.

DEBORA

King of the Fairies.

TAMARA

Very regal.

DEBORA

Yup.

TAMARA

I admire how comfortable you were with Joel's sexuality. Supporting his coming out and all that.

MICHAEL

He didn't come out.

TAMARA

What do you mean?

MICHAEL

He never, officially, came out to us.

BILL

Why not?

MICHAEL

How would I know?

BILL

You'd have been supportive?

DEBORA
Of course.

BILL
Strange he didn't then.

DEBORA
Would you, Bill? In high school?

BILL
I wouldn't know.

DEBORA
Would you come out?

CURTIS
In our school? Are you kidding?

TAMARA
You must've talked about it. Between yourselves. You must've known.

MICHAEL
Of course we talked about it. Somewhat.

DEBORA
It always made Michael uncomfortable.

MICHAEL
It didn't make me uncomfortable, I just—

    Beat.

We all have visions for our lives, our children's lives, and sometimes it's hard to let that go.

DEBORA

Course we're getting pretty good at that now.

MICHAEL

Don't forget he was our only child too. So, of course . . . that . . .

DEBORA

—in Michael's mind meant no father-son golf weekends, no Disney Cruises with the grandkids—

MICHAEL

Oh don't be so reductive—

DEBORA

Michael always wanted other children. But I said no; I needed some time for my art. But you were right. I can say it now. It's never wise to put all your eggs in one basket.

MICHAEL

We decided we would let Joel come to us when he was ready.

BILL

Which was going to be when, exactly?

MICHAEL

If we were going to talk it was going to be on his terms.

TAMARA

Did you ever have any general conversations about it? I mean around the dinner table.

MICHAEL

We didn't eat dinner together very often.

DEBORA

Michael talked about the Pride parade once.

MICHAEL

I have nothing against the Pride parade.

DEBORA

Except you didn't understand why they had to make such a show of themselves.

BILL

I agree.

DEBORA

I believe you used the term "circus animals."

MICHAEL

—that's out of context—

BILL

I mean you don't see straight parades.

DEBORA

Every day is a straight parade.

BILL

Ha!

MICHAEL

And Christ, it was four years ago and you keep bringing that up in conversation—

DEBORA

Well if I remembered it I bet he did.

MICHAEL

How do you think that feels for me when you bring that up?

DEBORA

Probably about as bad as it was for him to hear it.

TAMARA

You know, when we were young, people didn't come out like they do today. So and so would just have a roommate for five or six years and everybody understood what it was, nobody made a deal of it. They make such a fuss about it on TV / these days, no wonder kids think it has to be this big event.

BILL

Are you kidding? Of course it's a huge deal. It's a major life choice.

DEBORA

It's not a choice.

BILL

Well either way, it's a big deal.

DEBORA

I was always there for him to come to. He knew that.

BILL

Did he?

TAMARA

Of course he did; she's an artist.

BILL

Because I can see how if he felt ignored he might be tempted to get attention elsewhere.

MICHAEL
From bullies?

BILL
Flaunting his sexuality.

MICHAEL
Joel did not *flaunt* his—

DEBORA
(overlapping) Oh and of course all other boys keep their sexuality to themselves—

BILL
I would say the same thing about a girl wearing some microscopic skirt—

DEBORA
What, that she deserves what's coming to her?

BILL
No one *deserves* anything like that but we invite trouble / when we make ourselves vulnerable like—

DEBORA
(overlapping) I don't believe what I'm hearing—

BILL
(overlapping) No, I'm sorry, you are inviting trouble when you flaunt your sexuality; it's just the world we live in.

TAMARA
Deb, you have to admit he could be a little—extreme.

DEBORA
Tell me, what do you consider extreme?

TAMARA
Well some of his mannerisms, his attitude—

CURTIS
Saying: *(in fey voice)* "*Hey faggot*" to people. "*Hey faggot.*"

DEBORA
He said this? To you?

CURTIS
To everyone.

DEBORA
What was it about Joel that you hated so much?

TAMARA
I don't think that's a fair question.

CURTIS
I didn't hate Joel.

DEBORA
But something about him—bugged you. Was it that he was gay?

MICHAEL
We don't know that he was gay.

DEBORA
Michael . . .

MICHAEL

He never said it himself.

DEBORA

It doesn't take a rocket scientist.

MICHAEL

He isn't here to speak for himself and so I think out of respect for him /
we shouldn't begin—

DEBORA

Just because he never told you doesn't mean—

MICHAEL

You don't know!

DEBORA

Please, he was as camp as a row of tents!

CURTIS

I don't care if he was gay or straight or fucked goats or whatever; / he
was just weird and he tried to be. Like really hard. That's what was
annoying, that he tried to be a freak and did it in everyone's face.

TAMARA

(overlapping) —for heaven's sake—

DEBORA

Why was that so annoying to you?

CURTIS

He wanted the attention. So it's like, fine, we'll give him some attention.

MICHAEL
So you beat him up.

CURTIS
I never beat him up.

DEBORA
You smeared shit on his locker, Curtis. *You smeared shit on his locker.*

BILL
Okay—

DEBORA
No, it's not okay, this *(takes a handful of guacamole and wipes it onto the wall)* is not okay! *This is torture; you tortured him*!

CURTIS
(overlapping) That time wasn't me!

BILL
(overlapping) Get a hold of yourself!

DEBORA
You were there; they caught you at his locker; don't argue semantics with me, Curtis.

BILL
You are not in control.

DEBORA
Your son is not in control!

BILL

Do not shout at me in front of my son. And do not shout at my son, is that clear?

> *Silence.*

DEBORA

I'm sorry that was completely—I was out of line.

BILL

We agreed to boundaries. We were very clear about those boundaries.

DEBORA

I know; I'm sorry.

BILL

If you're going to ambush him, we're leaving. Is that clear?

DEBORA

Very clear.

BILL

Eh?

MICHAEL

Crystal clear.

TAMARA

Good, well everyone's clear clear clear, so let's just put it behind us.

DEBORA

Actually—

> DEBORA *picks up two shoeboxes from a table in the living room.*

Let's start. Let's just start. It's what we all came here to do. I feel like we're all ready to affect some, some change in this situation. Does anyone object to us just jumping into this?

TAMARA
Curtis?

CURTIS
Let's just do it.

DEBORA
I told Tam the best way to start, I thought, was through photographs. Michael thought that sharing some of Joel's awards—

MICHAEL
I want to share some of his successes with you. Because he always made me incredibly proud. He was really engaged. And going places. And so I just want to share some of his successes with you. Which, really, are so much more than can fit in a little—in this—

DEBORA
So we decided to do a little of both. A few awards, a few photographs.

MICHAEL
Should I just pass them to you?

TAMARA
One at a time, if you could. And tell us what they are.

MICHAEL
Okay.

> MICHAEL *opens a box and begins taking out medals and certificates, one by one, and passing them to* CURTIS.

Grade two Whiz Kid Reader Certificate. Grade three Whiz Kid Reader Certificate. The A.Y. Jackson Secondary School Medal for Public Speaking in grade six. This is a, uh, certificate he was given for participating in the Mars Lander Project in grade seven. Third-place ribbon for badminton in—I don't remember what grade actually, it doesn't say. Ontario Scholars Silver Medal for Academic Achievement in grade ten . . . and for grade eleven. These plaques are all course awards from high school: English, English, Family Studies, and Civics and Careers. Highest mark in his class. And this is a letter, which I framed, from the David Suzuki Foundation thanking Joel for his outstanding contribution to the environment. Which was, of course, for the composting program he started in high school.

BILL
Good student.

TAMARA
You know, we've been composting for years, haven't we?

MICHAEL
And those are just the ones I could find. I know there're others.

DEBORA
He had a couple boxes.

MICHAEL
He never let us hang them up though.

DEBORA
Very modest.

BILL
He was a big reader, was he?

MICHAEL *nods.*

DEBORA

So I've chosen five photographs that . . . capture Joel as I like to remember him. So I guess an obvious place to start: here's Joel's first photograph. That's me holding him when he's about three hours old. This is Joel's fifth birthday party. That's a lot of our family there. I was pretty happy with that cake; that's probably why this picture made it in because I'm still so proud of that stupid cake!

TAMARA

Oh, this guy was a big Thomas the Tank Engine fan too.

DEBORA

Well I gave it my best shot. This one is the three of us on the *Maid of the Mist* in Niagara Falls. I think the look on Joel's face speaks for itself. Not much more to say about that. Next is—oh this one's silly really. It probably shouldn't be in my top five, but here it is: Michael and Joel dressed up as George Bush and Sarah Palin for Halloween. What year was that?

MICHAEL

I can't remember.

CURTIS

Grade nine. I remember that costume. He still had braces then.

TAMARA

Oh that one's funny. Yeah.

DEBORA

And my favourite. It's at our cottage. The water was like glass. He was jumping off the dock and I took the photo just before his feet hit the water. Doesn't it look like he's just standing there on the water? I mean a second later and he's gone, but in that moment he's just hovering, looking right into the camera. Like he would stand forever and never go under.

CURTIS
So the letters now?

TAMARA
Did you want to go right into that?

DEBORA
We could wait for dessert.

BILL
No, let's just get it all on the table. As you said, that's what we came here to do.

CURTIS
Can you go first? I don't want to go first.

> MICHAEL *walks over to a drawer in the living room and pulls out an envelope and returns to the table with it.*

TAMARA
Oh you even got yours in an envelope.

DEBORA
Michael loves his envelopes. Every time he'd give Joel money for pizza day he'd put it in a little envelope marked "Pizza Day," and lick it closed, which was nice when he was in elementary but then I said to him, "The kid's in high school; he doesn't need your goddamn envelopes."

MICHAEL
Deb wrote this letter. I tried writing one but I couldn't.

DEBORA
It's true; he tried quite hard.

MICHAEL
It's just—I couldn't.

DEBORA
Okay. So . . . I'd just ask everyone to . . . open their hearts.

TAMARA gets CURTIS to sit up in his chair.

"Dear Curtis. These words do not come easily for me. And I can understand if they are not easy for you to hear. So to begin I just want to thank you for being here tonight and being open to embarking on this process of healing with Michael and me.

"On the night of March fourth, Michael and I were at a going-away party for a friend who was moving to Tanzania to teach English. Joel had often spoken to us about his desire to go abroad after high school. As we drove home, Michael and I talked about the wonderful places he could travel. How interesting it would be for him to see Africa, though how difficult it would be for us to be apart from him for so long. Luckily Joel had taught us how to use Skype last summer while he was away working as a counsellor at Camp Kawartha.

"When we arrived home I noticed the porch light wasn't on. I felt a little annoyed at this because I had asked Joel twice to leave lights on for us when we got home. But the whole bottom floor was dark. When we walked in and called for him he did not answer. I noticed his runners by the door so I knew he was home. He had been pulling long nights that week in the lead-up to exams so we figured he had already gone to bed. After all, it was going on eleven.

"We went upstairs to change in our bedroom. We were both in our pyjamas, and Michael was in bed reading, when I noticed the door to the bathroom down the hallway was shut. Being the compulsive person I am, I walked down the hall to open the door . . .

"And that is when I saw Joel sitting in the tub, just as if he were having a bath. I ran to him, but a large pool of blood had collected around the bathtub and I slipped in it and fell to my knees. And I held him. And I shook him. And I screamed his name over and over again. The boy who I held first, before anyone else in this world, the boy who I called my son for sixteen years—I tried to lift him out of the tub but I slipped on his blood and he fell—he fell—my own son lying on top of me—"

DEBORA cannot finish the letter.

I'm sorry I—here, just read it.

She hands the letter to CURTIS. *He begins to read it.*

TAMARA
Well. Read it.

CURTIS
I am.

TAMARA
So we can hear it.

CURTIS
It's meant for me.

TAMARA
Curtis.

"Joel breathed love and light into our lives. And now that light is gone. Many of his classmates came to his funeral, including you, Curtis. Many of them cried and had very kind words for us. And I know that for some, no matter where their lives take them, Joel will always have a place in their hearts.

"Curtis, my son's life was cut short by the vicious acts in which you took part. I know you alone are not responsible for Joel's suicide. But you were one of the hands that helped pull him away from us forever. For many months I harboured a lot of anger towards you and your friends. But I have come to realize that while there are evil actions, there is no such thing as evil people. And I do not believe, Curtis, that you are an evil person. I truly hope you go on to live a full life filled with family and friends who love and nurture you. I also hope you never forget the role you played in taking away what was most precious to me. But instead of it tormenting you, let it be a source of guidance and personal reflection. So that you may help prevent this tragedy from befalling someone you love, or someone you have never met.

"Every night I lay awake and think of the people Joel will never meet. The things we will never do. He will never graduate. He will never go to Africa. He will never fall in love. He will never get married, or have a job, or own a home, or grow old. He will never again ask my advice or opinion. He will never again tell me he loves me. He will never again kiss me goodbye.

"Sincerely yours. Debora Shaun-Hastings."

They sit in silence for a moment.

Would you like me to read mine?

TAMARA
Not yet.

BILL
That was very—touching.

TAMARA
Yes. Thank you.

DEBORA
I'm just going to get a glass of water.

> *DEBORA exits into the kitchen. They listen while she cries in the kitchen. TAMARA goes in to comfort her.*

MICHAEL
I just couldn't write one.

> *The three men sit listening to the kitchen dynamic. DEBORA and TAMARA return.*

TAMARA
Okay. We're all here with each other; we're all present. Deb, are you ready to receive Curtis's letter?

> *DEBORA nods.*

CURTIS
"Dear Mr. and Mrs. Shaun-Hastings. I've come here tonight to apologize to you both in person. My friends and I said and did things that I now regret. These things, that at the time were meant to be funny, ended up causing a lot of pain. Your son Joel was a classmate of mine and a lot of our jokes were at his expense. I apologize for the names that I called Joel. I apologize for posting mean things on his Facebook wall, and writing

mean comments under his YouTube videos. I apologize for being part of making a video imitating and making fun of Joel and for posting it on my Facebook wall. I apologize for being present as one of my friends rubbed feces on his locker, which I encouraged him to do. Whatever we did we did to be funny and did not expect to be taken seriously. We never thought about the consequences of our actions or that they might lead to Joel taking his own life. I am sorry for your loss and feel sadness about the part I played in it. And thank you for giving me the opportunity to apologize to you in person tonight. Sincerely, Curtis."

Beat.

That's it.

DEBORA
Did you write that yourself?

CURTIS
Yeah.

DEBORA
How long did it take you?

CURTIS
I had to think about it for a while.

DEBORA
And what did you feel, when you were thinking about it?

CURTIS
I guess I felt a lot of regret.

DEBORA
About what?

CURTIS

Well, about Joel killing himself.

DEBORA

And if he hadn't killed himself, would you still feel that way? If he was still alive.

BILL

I'm not sure how he's supposed to answer that.

DEBORA

Do you really feel—anything about this?

CURTIS

Course I do.

DEBORA

It just strikes me that your letter—it felt disingenuous. Do you know what that means?

CURTIS

I meant what I said.

DEBORA

Then why don't I believe you?

BILL

He's not an actor, all right, he just read the letter.

DEBORA

I'm not asking for acting, I'm asking for sincerity.

MICHAEL

And how're you supposed to judge that?

DEBORA

Sincerity, Michael, it's a human emotion. You feel it. I didn't feel it. I didn't feel anything, and *neither did he.*

TAMARA

I thought it was very thoughtful.

BILL

What'd you want, his head on a platter?

DEBORA

And where were you when all this was going on?

BILL

Where was I? I was at work, all right. I was at home; I was at the cottage. I didn't even know who your son was.

DEBORA

So you were just completely out of the loop.

BILL

And you knew exactly what was going on?

DEBORA

I knew there was a situation.

BILL

And what did you do?

DEBORA

I went to the principal.

MICHAEL

Who did absolutely fuck all.

DEBORA

He spoke to the teachers. He told me he spoke to the parents—

TAMARA

We were never called.

DEBORA

And Curtis was the worst.

BILL

Please—

MICHAEL

He was the chief instigator.

TAMARA

He never called us.

DEBORA

I tried to talk with Joel but he was very guarded—he wouldn't even tell his therapist about most of what was—

BILL

He was seeing a therapist?

MICHAEL

For depression.

BILL

Was he on meds?

DEBORA

That's none of your business.

BILL

Well that explains a lot.

TAMARA

Depression can be crippling. It runs in my family.

MICHAEL

It runs in every family.

TAMARA

Did you ever talk about that?

DEBORA

He was seeking treatment, of course we talked about it.

TAMARA

I just find this astounding. They never mentioned Joel's depression. Anywhere. The news, the school, / they didn't even—

DEBORA

Who's business is it?

TAMARA

I just—I'm totally astounded.

MICHAEL

She's astounded.

TAMARA

I just don't know why no one was talking about this.

DEBORA

Because it's nobody's goddamn business.

TAMARA

It's a huge part of the equation.

BILL

It's not as sensational a story.

TAMARA

It's not about being / sensational—

BILL

Or sympathetic, whatever. It's not! If people think it was inevitable.

MICHAEL

Inevitable?

BILL

If he had mental-health issues—

MICHAEL

You're right, you know; we decided to take it out of the press release because we were worried about compromising public sympathy—

TAMARA

I'm saying instead of sweeping it under the rug, why aren't we / having an open and frank discussion about—

DEBORA

Millions of people have depression, Tam, and aren't slitting their fucking wrists in the tub.

BILL

But some do!

DEBORA

I can't believe you're trying to use this as some kind of, of Get Out of Jail Free card.

BILL

And jail is *exactly* what this is—

TAMARA

I was just / trying to say—

BILL

These boys've already been tried by the press, the public, without all the evidence on the goddamn table—

TAMARA

When Joel was having a bout, did he ever open up to you / about what he was going through?

DEBORA

It wasn't a cold; he didn't have bouts of it.

BILL

So it was constant.

MICHAEL

He was a teenager! He sulked; he spent a lot of time in his room; he slept a lot—that's what teenagers do.

BILL

If you let them.

TAMARA

This is not about teen angst.

BILL
You can let your child shut himself away in his room and crank up the music or you can tell him to cut it out and interact like a normal human being.

DEBORA
Of course! We just lacked initiative.

BILL
I'm pretty sure people were depressed in the forties and fifties but guess what, stuff had to get done.

TAMARA
God, you sound like your father.

MICHAEL
I think he's right. We pathologize everything these days.

BILL
That's what I'm saying: excuses for everything.

MICHAEL
It's not about excuses; it's about reducing everything to a chemical reaction in the brain.

BILL
An excuse!

DEBORA
He was medically diagnosed by professionals.

BILL
And when you begin messing with the chemicals in your brain, things happen. Things can happen.

TAMARA

Bill, of course, has a degree in neuroscience. A real neuroscientist, aren't you?

BILL

It's not neuroscience; it's just common sense.

CURTIS

It's not neuroscience or common sense; it's psychiatry. You both sound like fucking morons.

BILL cuffs CURTIS upside the head.

DEBORA

Do not hit your son in my house.

BILL

Oh please, I didn't *hit* my son, it was a little smack.

DEBORA

Are you all right with him doing that?

TAMARA

He doesn't often, it's just—

DEBORA

Does he give you little smacks too?

BILL

For Christ's sake—

DEBORA

I want to know if you're comfortable with / your husband—

TAMARA

Did your parents never cuff you from time to time?

MICHAEL

Let's all try to calm down—

TAMARA

I think we all turned out just fine, thank you.

MICHAEL

I'm not so sure.

BILL

Listen, I'm not afraid to be a goddamn parent. And frankly, I think that's the problem right there.

MICHAEL

Not enough corporal punishment!

BILL

Tough love, Michael. We're raising a generation of wimps. That's the truth of it.

MICHAEL

Oh and was Joel a wimp?

TAMARA

No, that's not what he's—

BILL

He didn't know how to stand his ground. With other boys.

MICHAEL

You think this happened because Joel couldn't / stand his ground?

BILL

I'm saying maybe a little tough love from time to time wouldn't have been the worst thing in the world.

DEBORA

An occasional smack.

BILL

If my kid was walking down the school halls wearing eyeshadow you can be damn sure I would've given him a smack.

MICHAEL

Eyeshadow?

CURTIS

It was eyeliner.

DEBORA

I can't believe what I'm hearing.

MICHAEL

Neither can I—eyeliner?

BILL

He wore it to school.

DEBORA

Oh so what?!

MICHAEL

How many times?!

DEBORA

I don't know, maybe twice. Three times.

BILL
And you let him.

MICHAEL
I'm sorry, when was this?

DEBORA
Different times.

MICHAEL
And you never told me?

DEBORA
It didn't concern you.

BILL
(overlapping) I mean what did you honestly expect to happen?

MICHAEL
(overlapping) Damn well it does.

DEBORA
The fact that we're even sitting here debating this makes me sick.

MICHAEL
Did he ask you for this eyeliner?

DEBORA
I noticed it on him when he was leaving once.

MICHAEL
And you didn't stop him.

DEBORA
I do not have to sit here and justify anything to you.

TAMARA
He wanted attention.

BILL
Well that's obvious.

MICHAEL
And you would have straightened him out.

BILL
I would've sat him down and said, "Okay, buddy, so what's up?"

DEBORA
Hey Joel, what's up? What's up with the whole gay thing?

BILL
But of course ignoring him / is a much more enlightened approach.

MICHAEL
We were not going to make a big deal about his sexuality.

BILL
But it is a big deal!

DEBORA
Because people like you make it one!

BILL
The way you want the world to be, Deb, and the way the world really is are two different things. And you are a fool if you think being gay is no big deal out there.

DEBORA

The way I want the world to be starts in my house.

BILL

I'm saying talk to him honestly about what he's up against.

DEBORA

And you and Curtis sit down and have a lot of heart-to-hearts about sex?

BILL

We talk.

CURTIS

If I was gay?

TAMARA

Yes.

CURTIS

You think we could just sit around and talk about it?

BILL

I sure as hell wouldn't pretend it was no big deal.

DEBORA

Joel was different and that bothered you—because people like your father taught you to be bothered by it.

BILL

The bottom line is you should have helped Joel be better adjusted.

MICHAEL

By toughening him up.

BILL

I'm not talking about running him up and down steps Rocky-style, for Christ's sake. But if you're prancing around and flaunting it in peoples' faces you're making yourself a target.

DEBORA

Don't you understand what you're perpetuating? *(to herself)* Why am I even trying to—?

BILL

We're coddling our children to death.

TAMARA

Bill, choose your words.

BILL

Did you know you can be suspended for throwing a fucking snowball in the schoolyard?

MICHAEL

This is not about a few snowballs, Bill.

BILL

Have you played sports?

MICHAEL

I'm sorry?

BILL

Varsity, intramural. 'Cause you'd know that there's a certain amount of ribbing that guys dish out and guys have to take and that's just part of being young.

MICHAEL

It's not the Queen's rugby locker room, Bill; it's high school.

BILL

They're boys. Do you remember high school? Was it a walk in the park? Kids are cruel sometimes but you buck up.

DEBORA

Oh my god. You don't really believe Curtis did anything wrong. Do you? / You don't even think you're in the wrong. You think he maybe hurt some feelings here and there but it's all just boys will be boys to you, isn't it? Just toughening up a bunch of wussies who were asking for it anyways?

BILL

When you're posting videos of yourself on YouTube dancing around, dressed up like a woman, and talking about your classmates, you're asking for it, all right? That's just the way it is; you're asking for it.

DEBORA

What the hell are you talking about?

BILL

What do you mean, what am I talking about?

TAMARA

He sure as heck didn't help his cause by posting those ridiculous videos on the Internet.

DEBORA

Videos of Joel?

TAMARA

You don't know about the videos.

BILL
Jesus Christ.

CURTIS
There's, like, seven or eight.

MICHAEL
On YouTube.

CURTIS
Yeah, he's dressed up like a woman in some of them and doing stupid stuff like lip-synching to Rihanna or, like, one of them is a list of people he hates and wishes were dead—

TAMARA
—dead—

CURTIS
And he names like almost everyone in our class, their whole names and everything.

BILL
There's my favourite one—

MICHAEL
You have a favourite—

CURTIS
Oh yeah, the one where he has that wig on and he sings "Stay."

TAMARA
By Rihanna.

BILL

And he has that black stuff on his eyes—

TAMARA

Mascara—

CURTIS

He's crying, right, and it's all running down his face. But then he starts laughing at the end of it, like it's all a big joke.

BILL

He really has you going for a bit.

TAMARA

That one's a parody really. About how these pop videos can be. It's actually very funny. But they also get very serious. The cutting one.

DEBORA

Cutting—?

CURTIS

In one of them he cuts his face, like right here. But we knew he was faking it 'cause he showed up the next day and he like didn't even have a mark there or anything.

BILL

How could you not know about this?

DEBORA

Perhaps you should have invited us over to your little film festival.

TAMARA

It was all over the news.

MICHAEL
We avoided the coverage.

TAMARA
But Deb, this was front-page news.

DEBORA
Do you think I was out walking the streets? I was in bed twenty-four hours a day.

TAMARA
I mean here I was the whole night thinking you knew. So you have no idea how they painted my son and his friends out there?

MICHAEL
They're minors: they can't release their names or photos.

TAMARA
But how do you think Curtis felt being fingered as a, a, a *criminal* by everyone in his school: classmates, the administration, neighbours, our friends; we've lost friends over this. Lots.

BILL
Some.

DEBORA
I'm sorry to hear that.

TAMARA
But didn't you want to know details?

DEBORA
I knew the details. I held the details; didn't you hear my fucking letter?

TAMARA

Yes, but what about what people are saying? Don't you want to know /
what people are—?

DEBORA

Tam, I am a politician's wife. I've seen the parade. Scandals, deaths,
affairs. By the time the parade comes for you, you're so tired of it all that
you don't give a flying fuck what Christie Blatchford or Margaret Wente
has to say about your dead son. Really, I couldn't care less.

TAMARA

Obviously you care. You're taking more energy to avoid it than con-
front it.

DEBORA

Isn't this me confronting it? This seems pretty confrontational to me.

BILL

I just can't believe you didn't know about the videos. They're the crux of
the problem.

DEBORA

Can anyone see these videos?

CURTIS

They're on YouTube.

DEBORA

Still?

CURTIS

Till someone takes them down.

DEBORA
How?

CURTIS
You need his password.

BILL
You never wondered what he was doing in his room? He was filming them right above your heads!

DEBORA
Do you go snooping around in your son's room?

BILL
I know what my son does in his room.

MICHAEL
I'm sure.

DEBORA
Did his teachers watch these videos?

CURTIS
It's not like we hang out at each others' homes.

TAMARA
I suspect it was just among the students.

BILL
Everyone's seen them.

TAMARA
Bill—

BILL

It's the god-honest truth; everyone has seen them. It was all over the papers.

TAMARA

Again some of them are very fun. Very creative. But a lot of them are very—

BILL

Sad.

DEBORA

The last video . . . how long . . . did he make it before he—?

CURTIS

Like, maybe two weeks.

MICHAEL

"Just Another Bitch." That's what the last one's called.

DEBORA

I'm sorry, what?

MICHAEL

I read about them in an article.

DEBORA

You read about the videos in a—?

MICHAEL

I never watched them.

Beat.

Would you have?

DEBORA
I didn't even know about them a minute ago!

MICHAEL
Right.

DEBORA
What.

MICHAEL
Are you seriously telling me you didn't once google Joel's name or, or peek in the paper, or happen to flip through the channels / and see—

DEBORA
Fuck you.

MICHAEL
Would you have preferred I told you?

DEBORA
(to TAMARA) Would you? If you were me?

TAMARA
I can't say.

DEBORA
Say.

TAMARA
I hope I would've stopped him before they ever got on the Internet.

DEBORA
You kept these from me.

MICHAEL
I never watched them.

DEBORA
You just knew about them.

MICHAEL
I guess I assumed you knew.

BILL
But you watched the video the party made.

(to MICHAEL) You told me you guys found it touching. That oh so touching "It Gets Better" video your staffers slapped together; they never miss a beat, do they?

MICHAEL
That is so fucking cynical.

BILL
You ran that video like an ad campaign on TV.

MICHAEL
Excuse me? *I* ran / that video like an— Are you suggesting I—?

BILL
Every commercial break. They must've poured money into that thing.

TAMARA
All right enough.

MICHAEL

You think I was playing some sort of political game with my son's death?

BILL

Did they run it nationally?

TAMARA

This is not productive.

BILL

It practically had its own jingle.

MICHAEL

Unbelievable.

BILL

And I can't believe you watched that slick campaign but not the / videos of your own son.

TAMARA

She just said she didn't / know about the—

BILL

How could she not have—?

DEBORA

Bill, I never even opened the door to check the mail. We had raccoons because I left casseroles outside the door while Michael was in Ottawa; the neighbours complained.

She laughs.

A squirrel somehow got into the screened-in porch and died. The smell of its body filled the whole house—the curtains, the couch cushions—it would make you choke. I was in bed. I ate in bed. I cried in bed. And I would have shit in bed if I didn't have to do all the goddamn laundry myself because, let's face it, my husband has always been more interested in the spin than the spin cycle.

Silence.

BILL
All I'm trying to say is that it takes a village.

DEBORA
Please—unpack that sage tidbit for me, Bill.

BILL
I'm saying it's easy to blame one person when really there's a lot of ways in which Joel was let down. A lot of people let Joel down.

MICHAEL
You think we don't know that?

BILL
So don't lecture me.

TAMARA
They're not lecturing.

BILL
"Where were you; why didn't you know this was happening; why didn't you step in?" It seems like you knew less than anyone.

MICHAEL
It's not about fault.

BILL

Isn't it? You failed Joel. Not us.

TAMARA

Bill—

BILL

He was lonely; he was messed up; he / was confused, and he was reaching out. Anyone with half a brain could see that, all right, and it wasn't our job to reach out to him. And it's my son who's been raked through the mud!

DEBORA

Joel was not messed up—my son was *not messed up*!

TAMARA

Oh shut up, Bill, really just—

BILL

Coming crying to me at night— He can't sleep. He's not eating. Nightmares about the police breaking down his door, his teachers and neighbours coming after him, suspended for three weeks, that's on his record for life, and you're telling me this isn't about blame?

DEBORA

You have nightmares.

CURTIS

Yeah.

DEBORA

Often?

CURTIS
Every night.

DEBORA
They wake you up.

CURTIS
Yeah.

DEBORA
In a cold sweat.

CURTIS
A lot of them are the same.

DEBORA
Tell me one.

BILL
This is not—no. No.

DEBORA
If you can remember.

BILL
The point is—

CURTIS
There's one that I have all the time.

BILL
Curtis.

CURTIS

Starts with me in bed. And my room's dark. And I sense him below me. Not under the bed but . . . in the basement. He's in the basement of the house. And it's not like he makes a sound but I know he's down there. And he knows I know. I get up. And I walk down the hall. I walk down the stairs to the kitchen. I'm standing in the kitchen and I'm shivering. And I look across the kitchen at the basement door. I know I can't go back. I put my hand on the doorknob and I open it. It's pitch black. I smell the basement smell. I begin walking down the stairs. And I know he's there. I can feel him down there in the dark, on the other side of the basement watching me. I get to the bottom of the stairs and I'm moving towards him, towards the back corner where I never go. Until I'm standing in front of him. His back is bent against the ceiling. And his mouth . . . it reaches to the bottom of the ground. Like a seven-foot mouth. He is screaming but there's no sound—

DEBORA

What is he screaming?

CURTIS

I told you, it makes no sound.

DEBORA

You have this nightmare a lot?

CURTIS nods.

You should have nightmares. When you wake up in a cold sweat at night and you think someone is watching you, well it's me. I'm watching you. And that cold sweat on your body, those are my tears on your body—

TAMARA slaps DEBORA.

CURTIS exits into the kitchen.

92

Silence.

BILL
Now that was more than a smack.

TAMARA
You ever seen a bear trap, Deb? You just laid yourself out and waited for my son to walk in. You don't want an apology; you want blood.

DEBORA
Did you think you could just glide in here, tidy things up with this *(grabs letter)* this *(tears up letter)* and be home for that show of yours on CBC? Watch those designers be a real hoot together. Tell me: after they finish tying the curtains with ribbons do they share all the humiliating ways people like your son tormented them in high school? But no, what am I saying: it's only palatable if they're sashaying around spouting sassy quips about wallpaper. "I feel like I really get you, Deb." That's what you said to me. Well I know exactly who you are.

MICHAEL
Deb—

DEBORA
The kind of girl who giggles and shrugs. Boys will be boys! As they light dog shit on peoples' stoops or shout "faggot" from the car window. Now now, boys!

TAMARA
You don't know the first thing about me.

DEBORA
You're as complicated as a colouring book. Do you have any idea what it feels like to be tormented?

93

BILL

Oh I can tell you do.

DEBORA

Can you, Bill?

BILL

Oh yeah.

DEBORA

What, is it my pastiness? My haircut, my vocabulary?

BILL

It's your anger. That deep pit burning inside you.

> *CURTIS returns with an ice cube.*

TAMARA

What are you doing? Is that an ice cube?

CURTIS

For your face.

DEBORA

You carried it in your hand?

CURTIS

I couldn't find a towel.

TAMARA

You're not going to—

> *CURTIS puts the ice cube to her face.*

DEBORA
It must be cold.

TAMARA
Curtis—

CURTIS
It's almost gone.

TAMARA
She doesn't want cold ice / on her face.

DEBORA
Yes I do.

TAMARA
Put it down.

CURTIS
She said—

TAMARA
Curtis!

DEBORA
Let him!

TAMARA
I said put it down!

He stops icing DEBORA's *face.* TAMARA *looks at* DEBORA.

I didn't mean to hurt you.

DEBORA

Yes you did.

TAMARA

I'm sorry.

DEBORA

No you are not.

TAMARA

We came here with good intentions.

DEBORA

You came to be forgiven.

TAMARA

Forgiveness is the first step towards—

DEBORA

No, first come the blood and guts and tears, Tam, and you're not interested.

TAMARA

You're right: I'm not. I want us all to walk away a few pounds lighter tonight. Is that so wrong? After all this time?

DEBORA

Do you know what I'm going to do when you leave? I'm going to pick up each one of these plates, carry them into the kitchen, and load them one by one into my dishwasher with my son's body hanging around my neck. And you want to feel a few pounds lighter? All I am asking is for—

MICHAEL

For what? For them to cry for Joel? Throw dust in their hair? Do you want ululation? It's not their job to, to—

DEBORA

To feel?

MICHAEL

No.

TAMARA

We feel. Hold on, we *feel*. I'm sorry we are not quite so eloquent or if we don't watch the right television shows but we have felt this. I have felt this.

DEBORA

Then why do I feel like you are going through the motions?

BILL

Deb, let me tell you something about grieving. You can't talk your way out of it. And you can't share it with others. All right? It's yours to carry alone. And it's yours to carry forever.

Beat.

Can I be blunt?

DEBORA

Yes, let's try that for a change.

BILL

The first people you need to forgive are yourselves.

MICHAEL
Is that so?

BILL
Yes.

MICHAEL
For what, exactly?

BILL
For not knowing.

MICHAEL
The videos?

BILL
The bottom line is: you didn't know.

MICHAEL
I'm glad it's so simple for you, Bill. I suggest you follow that bottom line out of our house.

BILL
Well we agree on something.

TAMARA
Forgiving yourself is the most difficult thing in the world.

DEBORA
Oh stuff it, Tam.

TAMARA
It's Raj Gupta!

DEBORA

Is that how you got over your mother? Did you forgive yourself? Or did you just knit quilts until your brain liquefied?

TAMARA

There was a time there that I really thought—I really felt we were making some progress.

BILL

I take it we're passing on the pie.

MICHAEL

This was a mistake. I knew it would be.

DEBORA

How prescient of you.

TAMARA

We all knew this would be difficult.

DEBORA

Don't even pretend you know difficult.

BILL

I won't let you drag my family into your misery.

MICHAEL

Oh our misery is quite complete. Thank you. We have no room left for your family.

BILL and CURTIS rise from the table. TAMARA rises. MICHAEL rises to help them out.

TAMARA

This could have been a good idea. But you are both clearly not ready—I mean not even close—and you may never be, really.

BILL

I'm sorry for you; I am. I think you both need help. Serious, professional help. I don't wish any ill, though. If I pass you in Loblaws I'll say hi. Or in my car—

MICHAEL

Oh wouldn't that be nice.

BILL

—and I hope you do the same.

> *BILL and CURTIS are now dressed and ready to leave.*

Good night, Michael.

> *BILL extends his hand.*

DEBORA

Whoa, whoa, so this is it? Just like that?

MICHAEL

What, were you expecting the ref to ding the bell? Hold up the "Round 2" sign?

> *BILL pats MICHAEL on the shoulder with the un-shook extended hand.*

BILL

Let's get a move on.

TAMARA

I'll see you in the car.

> *BILL and CURTIS exit. TAMARA begins to dress into her outdoor wear.*

(to DEBORA) We're going to carry on with the rest of our lives. And I suggest you do the same.

DEBORA

I thought, for a while, we might have a shared loss. Mother to mother. But you don't know. You think you know, but you don't know.

TAMARA

I'm sorry this didn't work out.

> *Beat.*

DEBORA

Me too.

TAMARA

Well. The offer still stands for Curtis to trim that hedge of yours.

DEBORA

A few months of free hedge-trimming for my son's life. You run a hard bargain.

> *TAMARA exits.*

What a bitch.

> *MICHAEL and DEBORA begin to silently clear off the dining-room table.*

I can't believe you never told me.

Beat.

And thanks for all your support tonight. *Ululation.* You're so fucking clever, aren't you? If only you'd spend half that energy on even pretending to care about what I had to say instead of— Wait, shhh. There! Do you hear that?

A very faint knocking sound is heard.

That's the sound I was telling you about.

MICHAEL
I don't hear it.

DEBORA
Right there.

MICHAEL
The pipes?

DEBORA
Is that what it is?

MICHAEL
That *(imitates the sound)*?

DEBORA
Yes.

MICHAEL
Those are just the pipes contracting in the cold.

They listen.

DEBORA

I used to think that was Joel upstairs in his room. Do you remember that time I was in the kitchen and shouted up to him. "Sweety!" And you came in. You looked at me and said, "I'm right here." I made something up about needing help with dinner, but you knew. You knew I'd forgotten, just for a split second.

They listen.

There's so much I never knew.

MICHAEL exits. DEBORA breaks down crying.

After a moment MICHAEL returns with his laptop. He puts it on the table and sits down beside DEBORA. MICHAEL presses play. They watch a video of Joel singing Rihanna's "Stay," a cappella.

MICHAEL

They said this was the funny one.

DEBORA watches the video. After a moment she laughs in spite of herself.

DEBORA

I told you we should have put him in dance class.

MICHAEL

He liked the skating lessons.

DEBORA begins to laugh. MICHAEL begins to laugh with her.

Another knocking sound. At first they ignore it but it persists.
MICHAEL *and* DEBORA *look at one another;* MICHAEL *stops the video.*
The knocking is coming from the front door. Tentatively MICHAEL
rises, crosses to the door, and opens it.

CURTIS *stands in the doorway, crying.*

Blackout.

End of play.

A Polite Dramaturgy?
An Afterword for the Winner of the 2013 Herman Voaden Playwriting Competition

Can you imagine the sort of play Herman Arthur Voaden was looking for? The sort he hoped we'd perhaps find through the bequest he left to create our contest? A play that embodies the dreams and/or innovations he himself moved in the 1930s to create as a director-playwright with Group of Seven landscapes in his head and the non-naturalistic stage techniques of modernist Europe in his hands? And/or one that embodies the ideals or ideas of community the man served after the War, after we'd all seen what a fix folks over there got into, in his second career as a leader and activist for the arts here?

This play, any play—well-produced, well-attended, and attended to—might appear as an event, a ceremony. Among its other effects or affects, for those stepping hesitantly down the aisle into the theatre, escaping for a spell from the quotidian world, are pleasure, knowledge, order, or maybe even entertainment, education, healing. How practical, how useful, smile those whose diet is so much sponsored infotainment. But for those of us who are always, in spirit, on stage or just beside it, who take the art of playing seriously, that list shifts, becomes, we admit, ecstasy, vision, exaltation, yes, the stuff Herman Voaden, our benefactor, was on the lookout for.

Since 1997, biennially, round after round, we've been sifting through submissions, and our Voaden Playwriting Competition has found winners and honourable mentions; shadowed and illuminated dreams and innovations, often in subject; history remaking the world; stories of rural wilderness, of course, but also urban and international subjects, articulating, perhaps, the gentling forward edge of our Canadian essays at civilization.

Late Company, this winning play, evokes that most civilized of rituals—a dinner party. But it is one in which our urbane politeness proves a perhaps insurmountable impediment to an understanding of the causes of the suicide of a gay son, to his parents' ability to mourn. This sort of Canadian bourgeois politesse isn't easy—it's comic and sad at once—but it is human, worthy of remembrance in Mr. Voaden's name, yes.

—Daniel David Moses
for the Herman Voaden Memorial National Playwriting Competition
Queen's University
Kingston, ON

Acknowledgements

I would like to give heartfelt thanks to the many fine artists and institutions who shepherded this play into being. Peter Pasyk, Patrick Lavender, Rosemary Dunsmore, Richard Greenblatt, Paul Fauteux, Fiona Highet, Mark Correia, Emilie Aubin, Naomi Skwarna, Ravi Jain, Owais Lightwala, Why Not Theatre, the Theatre Centre, Andrea Romaldi, Incs Buchli, Matthew MacKenzie, Tarragon Theatre, Queen's University Drama Department and the Herman Voaden Playwriting Competition, Daniel David Moses, Craig Walker, Catherine McNally, Drew Dafoe, Marion Day, Steve Cumyn, Kyle Beres, Alberta Theatre Projects and the Enbridge playRites Award, Vicki Stroich, Laurel Green, Vanessa Porteous, Josh Dalledonne, Downstage Theatre and the Uprising National Playwriting Competition, Simon Mallett, Ellen Close, Paul Cowling, Kevin Rothery, Karen Johnson-Diamond, Barb Mitchell, Ryan Gray, the Consortium for Peace Studies at the University of Calgary, the Department of Drama and Faculty of Arts at the University of Calgary, the SummerWorks Performance Festival, Michael Rubenfeld, Touchstone Theatre, Katrina Dunn, Daniel Doheny, Michael Kopsa, Gerry Mackay, Kerry Sandomirsky, Katherine Venour, the Manitoba Theatre Centre, Steven Schipper, Camilla Holland, Sharon Bajer, Terri Cherniak, Daniel McIntyre-Reid, Doug McKeag, Cory Wojcik, Erin Brubacher, William Ellis, Jon Davies, Colin Rivers, and the Playwrights Guild of Canada. An extra special shout out to the hardworking folks at Playwrights Canada Press: Annie Gibson, Blake Sproule, and Jessica Lewis, and to Kris Knight for his beautiful painting. Finally, my eternal gratitude to my loving family: my brother Andrew; my parents Karen and Bruce; and my grandparents, Barbara and Keith, at whose home I wrote this play.

Jordan Tannahill is a playwright, director, and author. In 2016 he was described by *The Toronto Star* as being "widely celebrated as one of Canada's most accomplished young playwrights, filmmakers and all-round multidisciplinary artists." His plays have been translated into multiple languages and honoured with a number of prizes including the Governor General's Literary Award for Drama and several Dora Mavor Moore Awards. He is the author of *Theatre of the Unimpressed: In Search of Vital Drama* and the novel *Liminal*, published by House of Anansi Press. Jordan's films and multimedia performances have been presented at festivals and galleries such as the Toronto International Film Festival, the Art Gallery of Ontario, and the Tribeca Film Festival. From 2012 to 2016, Jordan and William Ellis ran the influential underground art space Videofag out of their home in Toronto's Kensington Market. In 2017, his play *Late Company* transferred to London's West End while his virtual reality performance *Draw Me Close*, a co-production between the National Theatre (UK) and the National Film Board of Canada, premiered at the Venice Biennale. In 2018, Jordan premiered his play *Declarations* at Canadian Stage, as well as *Xenos*, a collaboration with dancer-choreographer Akram Khan, at the Onassis Cultural Centre in Athens.

First edition: September 2015. Second edition: April 2018.
Printed and bound in Canada by Imprimerie Gauvin, Gatineau

Cover art, *Wilted Floral*, by Kris Knight, www.krisknight.com
Author photo © Alejandro Santiago

**PLAYWRIGHTS
CANADA PRESS**
202-269 Richmond St. W.
Toronto, ON
M5V 1X1

416.703.0013
info@playwrightscanada.com
www.playwrightscanada.com